POEMS
of the
HEART

Will Amacher

ISBN 979-8-89043-298-8 (paperback)
ISBN 979-8-89043-299-5 (digital)

Copyright © 2023 by Will Amacher

All rights reserved. No part of this publication may be reproduced, distributed, or transmitted in any form or by any means, including photocopying, recording, or other electronic or mechanical methods without the prior written permission of the publisher. For permission requests, solicit the publisher via the address below.

Christian Faith Publishing
832 Park Avenue
Meadville, PA 16335
www.christianfaithpublishing.com

Printed in the United States of America

CONTENTS

Cowboys for Trump 1
The Secrets to Liberty 3
A Virus Versus Our Anthem 6
Drain the Swamp 10
Who the Heck? 12
Jailhouse Love Letter 14
I Will Never Rest 16
Never Give Up 18
If I Were… 19
The "7 Aches" 20
To My Peanut 22
Dreaming of that Day 24
What Is Comedy? 26
A Heart of Comedy 27
Stand-Up Comic 29
I'll Write Your Name in the Sand 31
Lady in White 33
Lost Loved Ones 34
Moonlight Dancing 36
My Sweet _____ 39
Somewhere over the Rainbow 41
Spark of Love 43
My Vows to _____ 44
Stages of Love: Bride to the Groom 46
Stages of Love: Groom to the Bride 48
Starry Eyes 50
The Bride's Veil 52
The Sunny Flower 54
The Yellow Flower 55
I Need My Hero 56
I Gave Her All 58

I Dream	59
Happy Valentine's Day	60
Chosen Together	62
You're My Passion	64
You Are My All, Baby	65
Twinkle, Twinkle	67
To My Mom	68
The Eye on the Storm	70
What Is Holy?	72
What Is Joy?	73
What Is Hope?	75
What Is Grace?	76
What Is Faith?	77
What Do You Call Him?	78
'Tis the Season	80
The Call of Glory	82
The Altar	84
Thank You, God	86
Speak Life	88
Sow Is What You Reap	90
Run Your Race	93
Praise the Lord	95
OutLaws	97
One Passion	99
Not by Works	101
My Testimony: Will	103
No, No, No, No, No	106
A Husband's Prayer	108
Prayer of #1	113
Global Warming	115
America's Rebirth	117
I'm Coming Home	120
I Am Declaration	122
He Is Declaration	124

Ghost in the House	126
Generation Everyone	129
Come as You Are	132
Dance in the Fire	134
Bloodline	135
Blessed Salvation	137
Abortion	139
I Give	141
I Give You, Lord	142
I Hear a Sound from Heaven	143
I'm the Broken Clay	145
Jesus and Me	147
Love and Obedience	148
More and More	150
Mortals to Immortals	151
My God Is a Big, Big God	153
The Lord's Prayer	154
Sacrifice of Christ	156
Armor of God	159
Ask, Seek, and Knock	161
By Faith	163
Death to Resurrection	167
Great and Marvelous	170
Isaiah 61:1–7	171
No More Monsters	173
Spirit of the Lord	176
The Ministry Gifts	177
The Tunnel of Thoughts	179
Two Masters	181
You're the Salt	183
Blessed Are They	184
Speak the Word	186

ENCOURAGING

Cowboys for Trump

July 29, 2018
4:40 p.m.

there are many in the mountains
and there are many in the hills
we live and believe the blue
until we look our red pills
yes, we own ranches
yes, we own farms
and we unite against the blue
cowboys no longer be strong-armed
you raise our taxes
you steal our lands
you take bread from our tables
as you smash our hands
you lie and cheat
most of you, blue coats,
declaring your victory
while shoveling lies down our throats
well, the time has come
and the war has just begun
so run to your safe places
because now its gonna get fun
we have our guns
we have our hats
we have our horses

you, crazy loony bats,
we have our God
we have our rites
we have our President
we'll stand and fight
our voices we ring
to President Trump we salute
we're no longer being nice
from now on we are brute
for you have confused our kindness
by calling us weak
you tried to shut us down
by suppressing our freedom to speak
you call us Nazi racist bigots
you call us whatever
because your clueless insults
are no longer clever
I'm saying this loud
and I'm saying this clear
Cowboys for Trump
will always be right here
you wanted this war
with us it will end
you blue coats will lose
Do you comprehend?

    We are Cowboys for Trump

ENCOURAGING

The Secrets to Liberty

September 19, 2018
8:40 p.m.

I stand hundreds of feet
yes, I'm very high
I have my declarations
for you to reach to the sky
I stand by the waters
and I hold a large flame
I have a mighty voice
for this is what I proclaim
I'm a lovely lady
a lady who turned green
I have rules and laws
to some that may sound mean
my foundation runs deep
and my laws are my core
I stand for the rich
and I stand for the poor
I offer great freedom
and I offer a dream
I give hope to all
my dress has no seam
for those who see me
I give them great awe
the pursuit of happiness

I offer it to all
I give dreams to the dreamers
and give hope to the despair
yes, I know I came from France
with my long bronzing hair
as an ungodly symbol
to make America my home
but when I arrived here
I see God on the throne
I became a symbol
in this Christian land
I now represent
God's graceful hand
I'm now a Godly woman
who knows that God cares
my foundations were given
that freedom people do share
I stand before the King of kings
and for all his laws
my heart is a giant
and it's God's voice I do call
I am America's Lady
from sea to shining sea
God is our source
and that truth will always be
but as the Lady of this Nation
I do have to declare
that our Great Constitution
has to be enforced everywhere

we have to have rules
and we have to have laws
we as a Great Nation
must have border walls
there are no ifs
and there are no buts
we just can't let people in
that puts our Nation in ruts
there are many who do love us
but there are many who do hate
to confuse the two
would be a big mistake
a wolf is a wolf
and a fox is a fox
and to dress them as sheep
you put our safety outside of a box
we must stand united
and follow all our laws
because if we don't
our Nation will surely fall
there needs to be order
and we need to follow all the law
for if we turn a blind eye
Chaos will be our brawl
so you're either for me
or against me you stand
Freedom rings
don't bite the Lady's hand:

ENCOURAGING

A Virus Versus Our Anthem

January 27, 2020
5:57 p.m.

there is a virus
that's in the air
bounding people
in hate and despair
within its defense
bigotry lies
and racism gropes
in people's lives
there's yelling and screaming
and much name calling
there's kicks and punches
everybody's brawling
identity crisis
brings a new day
being homophobic
against the gays
being xenophobic
is what we are
carrying in our feelings
near and far
the spirit of delusion
has lifted high
self-importance

as we watch people die
we're in a place
where everybody is known
if we disagree
then we sit on a white throne
this ugly face
has many names
like white supremacy
privilege we gain
and if you're a man
then you are wrong
and in our Nation
you don't belong
and if you are dark
and happen to be white
you are where you are
and privileged in our sight
then there's the old
Nationalist cry
to our heritage
we all say goodbye
for we no longer have
a culture of our own
America stands helpless
as snowflakes groan
so forgive me
if I offend thee
let's be like the NFL
and let's just take a knee
or we can run and hide
to our Safe Space Zones
and cast out free speech

as we cast the first stone
or we can run to Mommy
and beg and plea
"Change my diapers
Oh, messy me"
Within this story
there's a message to hear
so gather around
yes, please do come here
for there is a virus
that's in the air
taking Liberty's Freedom
but don't be scared
for Freedom's bells
will begin to ring
as voices in America
will begin to sing
no more to the left
and no more to the right
we stand as one Nation
under God's sight:

Oh say can you see
by the dawns early light
what so proudly we hail'd
at the twilights last gleaming
whose broad stripes and bright stars
through the perilous fight
O'er the ramparts we watch'd
were so gallantly streaming
and the rocket's red glare
the bomb bursting in air
gave proof through the night
that our flag was still there
O say does that star-spangled banner
yet wave
O'er the land of the free
and the home of the brave:
    Never give up your right to freedom

ENCOURAGING

Drain the Swamp

October 17, 2017
10:50 p.m.

God is God alone
and Trump is only a man
and we will do our part
to drain the swamp out of this land
Washington has become very wicked
in all its child porn
and its involvement of witchcraft
it has become a thorn
in all of its dirty money
and the corruption of its mind
in all of its murderous theft
that surpasses all of time
the endless threats
that thrive in their hearts
in all of our corrupted leaders
is tearing America apart
we stand for unity
we stand for what is right
we chase wickedness away
back into the evil of its night
we claim our righteousness
we claim all our rites
we claim our country back

we will stand and fight
we chastise their sins
even in this hour
by the power of our prayers
we stand in greater power
we rebuke you, Washington leaders,
we stand by our man
President Donald J. Trump
that God has set in this land
you no longer have power of us
to you we no longer will jump
if you're against America
then you're just a chump
so whether you are a Republican
in your evil plans
or you are a Democratic
you will not bite our hands
because God is greater
than you and your sins
I promise you, both parties,
in the end we will win
God bless our President
in the draining of this swamp
you, America haters,
you we will surely stomp:

COMEDY

Who the Heck?

> February 14, 2015
> 11:36 a.m.

Who the heck
Is Amacher Will
That crazy guy
Over the age hill
He is an unknown person
And an unknown name
And he is a new face
But not new to the game
For those who don't know
Who this guy is
Let me introduce ya
He knows about showbiz
He's crazy in heart
And he's full of fun
He glorifies God
And he serves His Son
He knows about entertainment

And in its many forms
He's outside of the box
For he's not a norm
He writes poetry
And he writes songs
He doesn't smoke weed
In joints, pipes, or bongs
He writes books
And plays in skits
He tells comedy jokes
In his funny bits
So if you don't know him now
Have no fear
For comedian Will Amacher
To your town is coming near:

    Coming soon!

CHRISTIAN

Jailhouse Love Letter

> January 4, 2007
> 4:00 p.m.

Mom, you are awesome
And, Mom, you give rest
There are many mothers
But you are the best
She is a beautiful gift
That I will always cherish
My love for her
Will never perish
For to me
Mom, you're my guiding light
Shining through
The darkest night
And through my life
She's held my hand
And through her wisdom
Directed me in this land
And through her faults
She is never weak
She's like a battleship
That will not sink
I am proud of you, Mom
For doing what's right
Even if you're standing alone

In the heat of the fight
For your children love you
For you are the greatest mom of all
And don't let your dreams
To the ground crumble or fall
For we all do know
That man's law is not always right
But you always demonstrated God's law
The law of love, which is precious on sight,
RJ and I do love you, Mom,
Even if you're still in jail
Because this three-braided cord
Will never break or fail
For in the battle of every storm
We will always stand
Keeping our eyes on Jesus
For he is holding our hand
Love you, Mom
In God you have won
William Author Amacher
Your oldest son:

LOVE

I Will Never Rest

November 16, 2017
3:44 p.m.

This day I will declare
My love, I will never rest
As I sit here on the east
While your over there in the west

There are miles of ocean between us
My love, I will never rest
My heart aches for you only
But I know this is just a test

I may be without you for days
My love, I will never rest
No matter what troubles may come
Toward you I will press

And even though my heart aches strongly
My love, I will never rest
For you have given me great joy
That chases away all stress

And though the distance seems endless
My love I will never rest
For you have given me purpose
Yes, baby, you have given me a quest

As I long for your sweet presence
My love, I will never rest
I realize just how special you are
You're my hidden treasure chest

As my house sits empty
My love, I will never rest
And in our house, baby
You're my wife and not a guest

Baby, you are my world
My love, I will never rest
For you're not just my woman
But, baby, you're the best

Without you, life seems hopeless
My love, I will never rest
Because one day soon, we'll together
As your husband, I will stand blessed

As I long for that great day to come
My love, I will never rest
Because we are two love birds
Sitting and perching in our love nest

Baby, you make my soul whole
My love, I will never rest
Until your sweet beautiful head
Lays upon my tender breast:

    Baby, I will never ever rest:

Never Give Up

I will never give up
I will never give in
'Cuz, baby, I love you,
Deep within

I love you, baby
You drive me crazy
I love you, baby
Can't you see:

I will never give up
I will never give in
I will never take my ring off
'Cuz, baby, I love you deep within:

If I Were…

2021

If I were Cupid, I would shoot you with my arrows so you would fall in love with me:

If I were a turkey, I would sacrifice myself on Thanksgiving just to be with you:

If I were a New Year wine, I would age better in your love:

If I were a knight, it would be the greatest duty to be your servant of love:

If I were a king I would give you all my Kingdom for the Queen of my heart:

> These are just some examples,
> Of the man lives who in me,
> Who's totally in love,
> So all can see:
> My heart shakes,
> With overwhelming love,
> For you, my sunshine,
> My angel from above:

LOVE

The "7 Aches"

May 3, 2017
7:00 a.m.

Though I am a man
I'm so full of love
Toward my angel
That came from above
I'm so strong
Even in my hands
To carry my sweet love
Throughout the lands
My arms do ache
For my lover's tender touch
I say as a man
That I love her so much
A dim candle I am
She has a spark
Through her passion and love
She has set fire to my heart
My body does quiver
And my body does shake
At the thought of lovemaking
A child we will make
My mind is solid
On this very thought
That the love of my life

I, she has caught
My spirit is strong
And my spirit is weak
Without my love
Like a ship I will sink
My whole soul
Will never rest
Until your head
Lays upon my chest
These are the 7 aches
Of my entire life
With only one passion:
To be with my wife:

LOVE

To My Peanut

June 6, 2007
3:20 p.m.

My dearest baby
How are you
I pray all is well
In God's glorious dew
I miss you much
Each and every day
Wishing we were together
Walking the same way
I miss your smile
That shines on your face
And the sounds of your laughter
That pours out like grace
I miss your kisses
And all your hugs
I miss all your attitudes
And all your shoulder shrugs
I miss your child's way
And your playful heart

And singing our personal song
Of a love that will never part
Know this, my sweetest baby,
Your deep within my heart
And nobody, absolutely nobody
Will ever tear us apart
I love my peanut
And my peanut loves me
This is our song
That sets us free:

LOVE POEM

Dreaming of that Day

January 8, 2020

I went through the system
and I became free
and as I was standing there
my baby is all I can see
she bought me a ticket
and I went to the port
I boarded the plane
the trip was not short
I came to her land
right on time
there stood my baby
as I walked through the line
her arms open wide
as well as I
we both smiled at each other
as I looked into her eye
she said, "Baby, please kiss me"

I said, "I surely will"
it was at that moment
the world stood completely still
then from there
we went to our home
it was there in South Africa
our family did roam
the moral of this story
is how true I want it to be
to be with my wife and child
throughout eternity.

COMEDY

What Is Comedy?

*C*aring what you say,
*O*vercoming all your fears,
*M*anaging a laughable heart,
*E*arnestly seeking God's in your years:
*D*eliver a good message,
*Y*ielding and releasing God's joy,
    To every man and woman,
    And to every girl and boy:

COMEDY

A Heart of Comedy

The world of comedy,
Is made of all different colors,
We have some that are sisters,
And we have some that are brothers:
Comedy changes our emotions,
And talks to the heart,
Comedy brings us together,
Instead of tearing us apart:
Comedy has different languages,
But carries one voice,
Comedy is to lead you to laughter,
But I guess it's our choice:
Comedy has many forms,
And it has many styles,
Comedy can talk smooth,
While other talks are wild:
Comedy is for everyone,
Including those in the fight,
Comedy is design to make us laugh,

And that is our right:
So make all your laughs,
Out of all your tears,
Releasing your sorrows,
And all of our fears:
Let the life of comedy,
Release the pain,
Allowing pure joy,
Give you refreshing rain:
Press through the trials of life,
Let comedy be your heart's beat,
And before you know it,
All the hardship of life,
You will surely defeat:
And for goodness sake,
Let comedy flow from the heart,
And the laughter will come from the people,
As you do your part:
For God is a god of humor,
That's what comedy is to me,
And by the Spirit of Joy,
The people will be set free:

COMEDY

Stand-Up Comic

As a stand-up comedian,
It's a hard gig,
It's like standing in front,
Of a speeding rig:
The spotlights are on,
The floors are shiny,
And if you mess up,
You'll slip on your hinny:
The crowd is in pitch blackness,
As you make your jokes,
Hoping to God,
That you don't stumble or choke:
As you go through your bits,
You long just to hear,
The sweet sounds of laughter,
That breaks through every fear:
As I tell all comedians,
This is one simple key,
Just be yourself,
All you will be well receive:
And if they don't,
Then shake the dust off your feet,
And raise your head up,
And dance in the street:
Always be silly,
If that is who you are,

Because being in that character,
Will carry you far:
And my dearest friend,
Always have your fun,
Glorifying our God,
And glorify His Son:
For the joy of the Lord,
Is why you are there,
To bring people to laughter,
And out of their despair:
For God is a God of humor,
And the God of great joy,
So do your comedy bits,
And let the people enjoy:
For laughter is great medicine,
That heals every soul,
So let Jesus use you,
To make the people whole:

LOVE

I'll Write Your Name in the Sand

I will forever dream,
Of holding your hand,
As we walk along the beach,
I'll write your name in the sand:
As we travel the world,
From sea to shining sea,
Your name in the sand,
Will always forever be:
Don't worry about the waves,
That come crashing in,
Because your name is the sand,
I'll just write it again:
And please don't worry,
About the high or low tides,
For your name will always be in the sand,
Because you are my bride:
Don't worry about the marks,
Of the footprints you see,
For they are mine,

Of carrying you to me:
I'll write your name in the sand,
Whether far or wide,
And if your name disappears,
I'll write it in the sky:
And if too it dissipates,
Thank God for a restart,
Because your name will always be,
Written upon my heart:

LOVE

Lady in White

My precious bride,
My lady in white,
Living without you,
Just is not right:

I stand here today,
Only half the man,
My beautiful wife,
Until I hold your hand:

For you are my bone,
In you I am whole,
My love for you,
Is more pure than the whitest snow:

For we are royal,
I'm a mighty king,
To you, my queen,
I wed with this ring:

Your bone of my bone,
Flesh of my flesh,
Rib of my ribs,
I'm now bless:
    Your husband:

LOVE

Lost Loved Ones

I hear stories,
All the time,
About a lost loved one,
Who was once mine:
From the very start,
When we first met,
She changed my heart,
And made my heart wept:
She had no mom,
And she had no dad,
Although she had parents,
That's what makes this story sad:
So she changed my world,
And the way I see,
And even the shadow of her absence,
Is still changing me:
I am a better man,
Just because of her,
My eyes are now open,
And my heart she does stir:
Just the other day,
My heart matched my face,
I heard stories about her,
A sign of God's grace:
Oh, sweet child of mine,
I do hear your call,

It's ringing throughout my being,
Like a symphony's hall:
There's so much to share,
Even late within the night,
But know, my sweet,
You're worth the very fight:
So I close with this prayer,
That forgiveness will heal,
For God is a god of love,
And that truth is very real:
For you was sent from heaven,
A good gift from above,
I do pray for you child,
That God would show you my love:
For you will always be my child,
My lost loved one,
And at the end of this road,
Together we will run:

LOVE

Moonlight Dancing

Baby, it's all been real,
From the very start,
I knew you were the one,
Whom I love in my heart:
As we lift our glasses,
Of sweet-tasting wine,
Know that I'm all yours, baby,
And you are all mine:

We'll dance the night away, my love,
Under the moonlit shining sky,
Declaring our love for each other,
Beyond where angels do fly:

So here we are now,
I've been waiting so long,
To give you my heart,
Baby, to you I belong:
In different lands,
Honey, I can't wait,
To love and cherish you,
As we go out on dates:

We'll dance the night away, my love,
Under the moonlight shining sky,
Declaring our love for each other,
Beyond where the angels do fly:

Oh, I've been waiting,
For our two worlds to collide,
Our love is in front of me,
In which I will never hide:
My pounding heart says,
Baby, let's go home,
Where our beloved family,
Can live and roam:

We'll dance the night away, my love,
Under the moonlight shining sky,
Declaring our love for each other,
Beyond where the angels do fly:

We'll stand united,
As we marry,
You and I, baby,
Oneness we'll carry:
You'll be my queen,
I'll be your king,
My beautiful royalness,
You are my everything:

We'll dance the night away, my love,
Under the moonlit shining sky,
Declaring our love for each other,
Beyond where the angels do fly:

We'll fly away,
To build our lives,
I promise you, baby,
It will always be you and I:

LOVE

My Sweet _____

The stars do shine,
The universe is endless,
I long for your kiss,
I long for your tenderness:
The world is gigantic,
And lands of large masses,
My sweet _____ love,
Our two lives matches:
The ocean is so deep,
Wide is its sphere,
Oh, my sweet _____ love,
I wish you were here:
There are so many wonders,
That are easy to see,
Like the breath of life,
Like you are baby to me:
The earth has much glory,
And its beauty varies,
I found my bride's love,
_____ I do marry:
As air is so necessary,
And rainbows do point,
Oh, my sweet _____ love,
Us God has appointed:
The earth is awesome,
As it spins around and around,

I offer you my kingdom,
I offer you the queens crown:
The mountains show their splendor,
And it unfolds it's rolling hills,
Knowing your God's gift to me,
Gives me butterfly chills:
Each cloud forms its own charter,
As they float in being white,
Being with you is not just a calling,
But a destiny that sets the right:
The fields that stretches of so long,
Multitude of colors in their own beds,
You're prettier than all flowers, baby,
That's what dances through my head:
Oh, sweet _____ love,
I say this one, twice more time,
And I thank You, God the Father,
That you all are mine:

LOVE

Somewhere over the Rainbow

Somewhere over the Rainbow,
Is my pot of gold,
Somewhere over the Rainbow,
Is a person I desire to hold,
Somewhere over the Rainbow,
Is a precious stone,
Somewhere over the Rainbow,
Is a woman I call my own,
Somewhere over the Rainbow,
Is my shinning gem,
Somewhere over the Rainbow,
Is my family in Him,
Somewhere over the Rainbow,
Where all is beautifully green,
Somewhere over the Rainbow,
Is the woman of my dreams,
Somewhere over the Rainbow,
Is a woman just for me,
Somewhere over the Rainbow,
She's there waiting for me:

You're not going to find this Rainbow,
By sitting on your bed,
You're not going to find this Rainbow,
By voices running through your head,
You're not going to find this Rainbow,

By being overworked,
You're not going to find this Rainbow,
Until your life is shaken
Here's the point of this poem,
To all men who desire,
God gives you this Rainbow,
To lift you higher,
But you have to go and search,
Which the Scripture is clear,
You must leave your father and mother,
To your wife do draw near:

You must *go*...
You must *find*...
You must *search*...
You must *shine*...
You must *seek*...
You must *leave*...
You must *love*...
You must *believe*...

LOVE

Spark of Love

Baby, my love,
You opened up my heart,
You gave me life,
With one simple spark:
And, my sweetest babe,
It turned into,
a powerful flame,
Of loving you:
It's you and me,
Now I can see,
You saved me from myself,
That it will always be:
You saved me from myself,
Within my mind,
And, baby, my love,
You did it just in time:
I was a candle,
Who had lost his light,
But with your love,
Now I shine so bright:
_____, my wife,
You gave me a spark,
You're my purest love,
And that's straight from the heart:

LOVE

My Vows to _____

I can't help to think,
That diamonds you outshine,
Oh, my precious _____ love,
I'm so blessed that you are mine:
Oh, I can't wait, sweetie,
Until that precious day,
Where our world becomes one,
For Jesus is our way:
For our hearts are joined,
We are one in the same,
And I praise God the Father,
In Jesus's precious name:
For one day very soon,
I will take your glorious hand,
And at the end of the aisle,
My name you now carry in this land:
I will behold and love you,
For the rest of my life,
I will try to never cause sorrow,
Not even in hardship of strife:
I will love and cherish you,
For you are my precious bride,
I will not be a shame or bashful,
My love for you I will not hide:
I will guide and protect you,
Until eternity has no end,

My love will never wavier,
Nor break when it bends:
I will be your lighthouse,
To give you that shining light,
I will always stand beside you,
For you I will always fight:
I give you my world,
And I give you my whole heart,
I swear to you, baby,
My love will never depart:
Yes, you are my woman,
And I am your blessed man,
I thank God for joining us,
As we hold each other's hand:
So I announce on this very day,
As my kingdom's king,
That you will always be my queen,
For this makes my heart sing:
Baby, this is my hearts vow,
For every single word is true,
For I'm going nowhere my wife,
I'm spending my complete life with you:

LOVE

Stages of Love: Bride to the Groom

I do know you,
And you look so good,
Being here in your presence,
Makes me feel like I should:
When we first met,
And fell in great love,
We became two peas in a pod,
Like hand in glove:
And together we will grow,
A great love in my heart,
For you are no longer my boyfriend,
And together we will never depart:
Then we will see the wedding bells,
And make our vows to each other,
For this will be the time,
To leave our father and mother:
We will fly in unity,
Holding hand in hand,
Soaring to the altar,
As couples we now stand:
You stand as my groom,
And I stand as your bride
Our love for each other,
We will never hide:
We are #1 in soul,
We are #1 in our heart,

The arrows of our loins,
We pierce like darts:
Our family love,
Will never run dry,
Because within our vows,
Together we will die:
And if that day ever comes,
To bring this dream to an end,
I speak to you, my dearest husband,
My dearest closest friend:
Our great love for each other,
I will take to the grave,
So look up to the heavens,
My husband, do be brave:
I will wait for you in heaven,
The angels and I are singing,
Through the love they had for each other,
Soon him the Lord will be bringing:
For these are the stages,
One of the greatest love,
I want to grow old with you,
My husband, my angel dove:

LOVE

Stages of Love: Groom to the Bride

I do know you,
And you are beautiful,
Being here in your presence,
Makes me so thankful:
When we first met,
And fell in great love,
We became two peas in a pod
Like hand in glove:
And together we will grow,
A great love in my heart,
For you will no longer be my girlfriend,
And together we will never depart:
Then we will see the wedding bells,
And make our vows to each other,
For this will be the time,
To leave his father and mother:
We will fly in unity,
Holding hand in hand,
Soaring to the altar,
As couples we now stand:
I stand as your Groom,
And you stand as my Bride,
Out love for each other,
We will never hide:
We are #1 in soul,
We are #1 in our hearts,

The arrows of our loins,
We pierce like darts:
Our family love,
Will never run dry,
Because within our vows,
Together we will die:
And if that day comes,
To bring this dream to an end,
I speak to you my beautiful wife,
My dearest closest friend:
Our great love for each other,
I will take to the grave,
So look up to the heavens,
My wife, do be brave:
I will wait for you in heaven,
The angels and I are singing,
Through the love that they have for each other,
Soon her the Lord will be bringing:

For these are the stages,
One of the greatest love,
I want to grow old with you,
My wife, my angel dove:

LOVE

Starry Eyes

There are many stars,
In the midnight skies,
But there is only one,
Who gives me starry eyes:
Her garment is white,
Her garment is clean,
With pure love,
She makes me beam:
There is a light,
She's like the moon above,
She clothes me with joy,
She clothes me with her love:
There is a great warm ray,
She's like the sun,
Her and I together,
We are truly #1:
But as I look,
And I see my star,
In my heart,

She's never far:
Even through there are many miles,
That stand between you and I,
But you, sweet _____,
You're the apple of my eye:
This beautiful woman,
I ask not God the whys,
I just know that my wife,
Gives me starry eyes:

LOVE

The Bride's Veil

Wow, the day has come,
And I stand here as a man,
Waiting for my bride,
Because I asked for her hand:
I'm here at the altar,
Looking down the aisle,
I've been waiting for his moment,
I've been standing here for a while:
My nerves are very high,
And my heart is beating harder,
As I stand in Jesus,
And under God our Father:
Here I stand now,
I see you coming toward me,
I'm reminded of our love,
That sets us both free:
As you stand in front of me,
And my body does shake,
This is our priceless moment,
In each other we do take:
The preacher does his quotes,
Line after line,
Where I'm forever yours,
And you are forever mine:
I put a ring on your finger,
And you put one on mine,

Resemblance of our undying love,
Until the end of time:
Now we are at the point,
Where he declares us as #1,
Under the Holy Spirit,
And under God and his Son:
As I reach toward the veil,
To kiss my beautiful bride,
My love for you, baby,
I will never hide:
You are now my wife,
And I'm now your husband,
Just like our circle rings,
Our marriage will never end:
I love you, honey,
For this I declare,
We belong to each other now,
In our love and prayer:

LOVE

The Sunny Flower

Poems are many,
Poems are few,
But I write this poem,
Just for you:
The Sunny Flower,
Is a symbol of you,
As your array of beauty,
Falls like glorious dew:
As the seasons come,
And the flower hides,
My Sunny Flower,
I will stand by your side:
So as the New Year unfolds,
Keep the joy inside,
Because one day soon,
You and I will collide:

LOVE

The Yellow Flower

Poems are many,
Poems are few,
But I write this poem,
Just for you:
All Yellow Flowers,
Release a deep joy inside,
You array of beauty,
You should never hide:
So as the New Year turns,
And beauty is in the eye,
Know you're a shining star,
In the midnight skies:
And you will never die,
Because of your seeds,
For you will keep growing back,
Because you the world needs:
So oh, Yellow Flower,
You are well loved,
For over all other flowers,
You stand far above:

LOVE

I Need My Hero

I need my hero,
for the night,
I've been around the globe,
And seen the light:

I need my hero,
For the night,
I see my wife,
Who's dressed in white:

I need my hero,
For the night,
I need you, _____,
For you are my right:

I need my hero,
For the rest of my life,
She's a glorious queen,
Yes, she's my wife:

I need my hero,
Until I die,
Our love for each other,
Reaches beyond the skies:

Yes, my honey,
You are my hero,
I love you, babe,
In you I'm no longer a zero:

LOVE

I Gave Her All

I gave her money,
I gave her time,
I gave her everything,
Including my last dime;

I gave her my bike,
I gave her my car,
I gave her my dreams,
Of lands from afar:

I gave her my hand,
I gave her my keys,
I gave her my heart,
As she pleases:

The point of this poem,
Is to let the world know,
Our love for each other,
I pray will always grow:

LOVE

I Dream

With my lips to yours,
You are the joy of my life,
Arise up, oh, God,
In my beautiful wife:

Every day in my prayers,
Every day in my cries,
You are my beautiful wife,
You're the apple of my eyes:

I long to be your husband,
I long to be a dad,
To the greatest wife and son,
You both make my heart glad:

I dream in the day,
And I dream in the night,
I dream of holding you, baby,
In my arms, oh, so tight:

I dream of your kisses,
I dream of getting old,
With you, my sweet darling,
My treasure, my gold:
Your husband,

_____

LOVE

Happy Valentine's Day

The touch of your skin,
Is my desire within,
Only with you, baby,
In life can I win:

I share what I feel,
You are my meal,
My heart you steal,
My love for you is real:

The sex will be great,
Beyond our first date,
With you I will mate,
Together we will create:

Here's the point,
Us, God has anoint,
You I will never disappoint,
Together we're #1 joint:

Yes, I am your man,
Your husband in this land,
Together we will stand,
So, baby, take my hand:
You I do pursue,
We are #1 not #2,
For I love you,
And this love is so true:

Happy Valentine's Day, my wife…
    Your husband, _____

LOVE

Chosen Together

As a little boy,
I had many dreams,
Growing up in the heartlands,
Of rivers and streams:
My daddy was great,
And so was my mom,
Through their problems,
It seemed like fire bombs:
I grew up in a life
That wasn't very fair,
But I had only one dream,
That I really do care:
I wanted to marry a princess,
Not in some fairytale,
I wanted something tangible,
I wanted something real:
I thank God for saving me,
And making me a king,
I thank God for His timing,
Because now I can sing:
I sing this song in the valleys,
I sing this song in the hills,
That He has given me a queen,
Whose love I can feel:
I praise His very name,
Who chosen me for you,

Who called us together,
To walk as a chosen few:
I glorify Him every day,
For chosen you for me,
Babe, you're such a wonderful gift,
Together we will always be:
Yes, darling, you're my queen,
And I will always be your king,
Together we will glorify God,
In our everything:
I am your gift, baby,
And you are mine,
Together we are chosen,
Until eternities end of time:

LOVE

You're My Passion

Let's not let our words,
Past each other,
In the very distance,
Which is a bother:
Baby, you deserve all,
To grow and to shine,
To know you're out there,
And to know you're mine:
My heart dreams of much,
As I walk through the lands,
It is my one desire,
To one day hold your hands:
My passions are beyond sex,
My passions are so true,
Before God's altar,
My passion is for You:
So as your husband,
I say this loud and clear,
So all the nations hear,
Baby, I love only you:
  Your husband, _____

LOVE

You Are My All, Baby

You are my *angel*,
Sent from above,
You are my *angel*,
My earthly love:
You are my *angel*,
My only desire,
You are my *angel*,
Who lifts me higher:

You are my *sunshine*,
Who makes me grow,
You are my *sunshine*,
I desire to know:
You are my *sunshine*,
Over the rainbow,
You are my *sunshine*,
My treasure flow:

You are my *bride*,
My woman in white,
You are my *bride*,
My life's delight:
You are my *bride*,
My very heartbeat,
You are my *bride*,
Who swept me off my feet:

You are my *queen*,
Who rules beside me,
You are my *queen*,
Together we stand free:
You are my *queen*,
In our kingdoms reign,
You are my *queen*,
In Jesus's name:

You are my *wife*,
Yes, we are #1,
You are my *wife*,
In Jesus the son:
You are my *wife*,
We are firm in our vows,
You are my wife,
All else bows:

LOVE

Twinkle, Twinkle

Twinkle, twinkle,
Little star,
How I know,
You are far:

Twinkle, twinkle,
You're so near,
In my heart,
I do not fear:

Twinkle, twinkle,
When I close my eyes,
I vow to you,
There'll never be goodbyes:

Twinkle, twinkle,
Brightly do shine,
Because, my love,
You're all mine:

Twinkle, twinkle,
Oh, how I love thee,
My sweet love,
It will always be you and me:

LOVE

To My Mom

Moms are awesome,
Moms are the best,
But my mom
Stands far above the rest:
She is a God-given gift,
That I do cherish,
Our love for each other,
Will never die or perish:
For she to me,
She's a guiding light,
Shining in her strength,
In the darkest night:
And through my life,
She's held my hand,
And through her wisdom,
Guided me in this land:
And in her faults,
She was never weak,
She's like a battleship,
That just won't sink:
I'm proud of my mom,
In what she is doing,
Trusting in God,
And Him she's pursuing:
She knows His will,
And what is right,

Standing in the Lord,
And in the power of His might:
I do love you, Mom,
For being greater than all,
Holding me up in your prayers,
So I would not crumble or fall:
But most of all,
Do not let die,
The Christ within you,
Because you're the apple of His eye:
So I thank you, Mom,
For doing your part,
Becoming my mom,
And sharing your heart:

ENCOURAGING

The Eye on the Storm

In everyday life,
There are ups and downs,
There are joy and smiles,
And there are sadness and frowns:
The storms of life don't care,
What color skin you are,
The storms of life don't care,
If you are near or far:
For it rains on the unjust,
And it rains on the just,
But what makes the difference,
Is where you put your trust:
So when the storms of life come in,
In its mighty powerful rage,
Turn to the Lord Jesus Christ,
He'll help you turn the page:

For no one is exempt,
When the storms do hit,
Let Jesus control the hem,
So your ship won't flip:
For He said walk on the waters,
By taking His hand,
And you'll see the storms cease,
At the voice of His command:
For His eye is on the storm,
Because He watches over you,
Trust only in Jesus Christ,
He will see you through:

ENCOURAGING

What Is Holy?

*H*onoring God in everything we do,
*O*beying Him no matter what you heard,
*L*iving by faith in God alone,
*Y*ielding fruits of His Word:
    For to be holy,
    Is something you can't do on your own,
    Not even your friends can help you,
    Even if you do have a cell phone:
    So if you want to be holy,
    There is only one way,
    And that's to ask a holy God,
    To come in you to stay:
    So rid your thoughts,
    And rid your sins,
    Ask upon the Lord Jesus Christ,
    That's the only way you'll be cleansed:
    There is none righteous or holy,
    Other than Jesus Christ the Son,
    So for mankind to be holy,
    In Jesus Christ we must be One:

ENCOURAGING

What Is Joy?

We all heard this simple truth,
I know it sounds very absurd,
But it really doesn't matter,
What you have heard:
    J is for *Jesus*,
    O is for *others*,
    Y is for *yourself*,
In this truth, don't smother:
It is a simple rule,
So follow it to the T,
And though you may have friends,
Jesus the people will see:
The first simple rule is,
Always keep this in mind,
Love the Lord Jesus Christ,
And you'll always will shine:
Ho, ho, ho,
Some may say,
But loving others,

Blesses the day:
Now for the third part,
Which lastly is you,
When you follow the upper two,
You'll have a joyous dew:
So live in *joy*,
And you'll always have fun,
And you'll experience real joy,
Under the earth's sun:
Always do remember,
This is straight from the heart,
Keep Jesus, others the you,
For this is where real joy starts:

ENCOURAGING

What Is Hope?

Hope is…
*H*aving faith in God,

Being…
*O*vercomers of all,

And endurance by…
*P*ressing through to the very end,

Knowing…
*E*ternity trusting in Him we'll never fall:
    So from hope,
    You'll never become weak,
    Fall to your knees,
    And God do please seek:
    For He knows our hearts,
    And He knows our prayers,
    Hope is knowing that God,
    Will always be there:

ENCOURAGING

What Is Grace?

Grace is…
*G*rowing in God,

Being…
*R*ighteous in Jesus Christ,

Having…
*A*ssurance in His love,

Knowing…
*C*hrist Jesus paid the price:

Thanking…
*E*very day in our lives,
    We need to thank and give God praise,
    For it's not by works,
    But by God's amazing grace:

ENCOURAGING

What Is Faith?

*F*oundation in Jesus Christ,
*A*ssurance in God,
*I*mparting truth against negative,
*T*rusting always in God's Word,
*H*aving what you believe for:

Faith only comes,
By hearing the Word,
And hearing the Word of God,
To it you can *always* referred:

ENCOURAGING

What Do You Call Him?

Some may call Him Prophet,
Some may call Him King,
Some may call Him Lord,
Who's over everything:

Some may call Him Brother,
Some may call Him Man,
Some may call Him Savior,
Who saves in this land:

So what do you call Him,
In your life?
Is He your God?
Is He your Christ?

What do you call Him,
In your life?
Is He your God?
Is He your Christ?

Some may call Him Master,
Some may call Him Lamb,
Some may call Him Jesus,
Who is the Great I am:

Some may call Him Teacher,
Some may call Him Son,
Some may call Him Christ,
Who is the only One:

So what do you call Him,
In your life?
Is He your God?
Is He your Christ?

What do you call Him,
In your life?
Is He your God?
Is He your Christ?

ENCOURAGING

'Tis the Season

Every signal year,
There comes a day,
Some call it Christmas,
Santa on his sleigh:
The weather turns cold,
And snow lays on the ground,
It's a celebration time,
As you see lights all around:
Stars and angels hanging high,
On top of pine trees,
Wreaths hanging on doors,
In the winter breeze:
Colors fill the sky,
Frost in the air,
Gifts are given,
To people we care:
Joy is released,
As families do gather,
Laughter is heard,
As sadness is shattered:
Peace is shared,
As a star shines bright,
Celebrating the birth of Jesus,
The true King of light:
From my heart to yours,
Merry Christmas day,

Knowing that Jesus Christ,
Is he only light and way:
So while you gathering,
Around the fireplace,
Remember the hurting,
See their lonely face:
If you are alone,
Always remember,
God sits on the throne:
He will never leave you,
Nor will He forsake,
Because in His eyes,
You are no mistake:
As for you, my friends,
This Christmas you share,
With friends and family
Whom you keep in prayer:
Know it's not about,
Who can push and shove,
But it's all about,
Showing God's love:
There is no greater love
Than what God has done,
Sending His only beloved,
Jesus Christ the Son:
So as you drink your hot cocoa
In this holiday season,
Never forget,
Jesus is the reason:
Merry Christmas

ENCOURAGING

The Call of Glory

I'm all shaken up,
To say that all of man,
Is full of wickedness,
And spread evil in this land:
But there is a way out,
Of this evil and sin,
His name is Jesus Christ,
So do ask Him in:
See God is bigger,
And He does have a plan,
To make you His child,
To give you His brand:
So once you are His,
Satan you can beat,
Not because of yourself,
But Jesus sits the seat:
See every one of us,
Was born into sin,
And every one of us,
Needs to ask Jesus in:
See every one of us,
Has been called,
To give God glory,
Even if we have to crawl:
See we were made in His image,
And to glorify His name,

Because it was Jesus,
Who took our guilt and shame:
Do not be self-centered,
Or be high-minded,
And lean not in your own understanding,
Or from Him be divided:
For it was God the Father,
Who sent His Son,
So we in Him,
Can all be one:
Here's the point of this poem,
All of us has a call,
To give God glory
So to your knees do fall:
In every situation,
Whether high or low,
Glorify our God,
For His mercy does show:

ENCOURAGING

The Altar

There is a place,
That is very real,
It's waiting for you,
And no one can steal:
It's called the altar,
Where there is grace,
And there is forgiveness,
There you'll see His face:
There you'll be in His arms,
Which is open wide,
And just like the birds,
He'll gather you by His side:
No matter who you are,
Or what you have done,
There is forgiveness,
Through Jesus the Son:
No matter what you look like,
Or the deepness of your sin,
The power of Jesus blood,
Will cleanse you within:
So come to the altar,
That stands before the cross,
For Jesus did come,
To seek and save the lost:
His arms are open wide,
And He's waiting for you,

To ask Him for forgiveness,
And become a part of His crew:
There is no sin to great,
And there is no sin to small,
For the precious blood of Jesus,
Can wash them *all*:
Come to this altar,
And heed to His call,
Harken unto the Father,
To your knees do fall:
Cry out to the Father,
And ask Jesus Christ in,
Because when you do,
You'll become born again:

ENCOURAGING

Thank You, God

Thank you, God,
I am now free,
Thank you, God,
For living in me:
Thank you, God,
That Christ is He,
Thank you, God,
It's now we:
Thank you, God,
In you I glee,
Thank you, God,
Your truth shall be:
Thank you, God,
I am a tree,
Thank you, God,
Your Word I decree:
Thank you, God,
For the victory,
Thank you, God,

For dividing the sea:
Thank you, God,
The storms cease,
thank you, God,
I trust in thee:
Thank you, God,
There's no disease,
Thank you, God,
You I please:
Thank you, God,
I have heavens keys,
Thank you, God,
Now I can see:
Thank you, Father God

ENCOURAGING

Speak Life

There is a truth,
In what I say,
What you speak,
Will make your every day:
For the Bible,
Makes it clear,
What you value,
Is what is dear:
Life or death,
Are in your tongue,
Please chose life,
Rather than the wrong:
What you speak,
Releases power,
Cursings or blessings,
On you will shower:
Out of your heart,
The month speaks,
This does define,
You're strong or weak:
For it has been said,
From the time of old,
Either you are free,
Or have been sold:
It's not what comes in,
But that which goes out,

That makes you defeated,
Or gives you the shout:
As Jesus said,
If there was a glass,
If water's afresh,
The salt makes it clash:
The water's not fresh,
Because of the salt,
It's now worthless,
Is the end result:
So speak the Word,
Speak life within,
Chasing out death,
You'll always win:

ENCOURAGING

Sow Is What You Reap

On my bed,
Is where I sleep,
On my knees,
Is where I weep:
In my car,
Is how I drive,
On my feet,
Is how I arrive:
In my head,
Is how I think,
Through my mouth,
Is how I drink:
We as people,
Need to realize,
We reap what we sow,
It shouldn't be no surprise:
If we sow,
The seeds of hate,
We become pawns,
To satan's bait:
If we sow,
Seeds of discords,
Then with hell's crowd,

We become one accord:
If we sow,
The seeds of deceit,
In the walls of separation,
We're ten at satan's feet:
If we sow,
The seeds of unforgiveness,
We also sow the seed of envy,
Without righteousness:
If we sow,
The seeds of sexual sin,
Then we take away,
The priceless jewels within:
If we sow,
The seeds of greed,
Then the seed of jealousy,
Has it's needs:
The moral is,
of what I'm trying to say,
The seeds we sowed yesterday,
Is what we will reap today:
It may take hours,
Or it may take years,
We will reap what we sow,

For that is abundantly clear:
So listen to my words,
And renew our thoughts,
And sow the seeds of holiness,
For our minds have been bought:
Bondage to the lies,
From the very start,
Sowing seeds of unrighteousness,
That breaks God's heart:
So listen, my friend,
Be careful of what you do,
For what so ever you sow,
You will one day reap too:

ENCOURAGING

Run Your Race

The Bible tells us,
To run our own rave,
But to every marathon,
You must set your pace:
This means you have to choose,
To be very wise,
So at the very end,
You can win your prize:
There are going to be,
Many road blocks,
So run with the Word,
Instead of in your socks:
And there are going to be,
Man swallowing potholes,
But look unto Jesus,
The Author and finisher of your goals:
And there are going to be,
Many, many wrong turns,
But be filled with the Spirit,
So you'll never get burned:
And there are going to be,
Lies spoken against your heart,
But put on the armor of God,
So you can stand those evil darts:
And there are going to be,
Things that will cause you to stumble,

In yourself be not prideful,
But in Him always be humble:
And there are going to be,
People who cause you to despair,
But cast all your burdens to Him,
For you He does care:
And there are going to be,
Sadness and broken hearts,
But in His will,
Pray to Him and be smart:
And there are going to be,
Natures forces against you,
That will cause you to tumble,
Yes, this is what you need to do:
Set your eyes on Jesus,
And follow His every Word,
Listen to His Holy Spirit,
So your vision doesn't become blurred:
Remember this wise statement,
Always set your course,
So at the end of your race,
You wouldn't ever have remorse:
You are the victor,
Of your God-given race,
But know it's not by your might,
But by God's awesome grace:

ENCOURAGING

Praise the Lord

Praise the Lord,
And His holy host,
He's filled us,
With His Holy Ghost:

Run into my arms tonight,
Together we will stand and fight,
I sing unto you a brand-new tune,
That Jesus is coming back soon:

So with your voice do declare,
We're united in this hemisphere,
We're a might warriors in Him,
We're His Royal Diadem:

So run into His arms tonight,
For the battle is His to fight,
We're kings and we're His queens,
While all of heaven does sing:

Praise the Lord,
And His holy Host,
He's filled us,
With His Holy Ghost:
So praise the Lord,
And His holy Host,
He's filled us,
With His Holy Ghost:

ENCOURAGING

OutLaws

There are many rules,
And there are many laws,
Most of them are dangerous,
For their there to cause people to fall:
Yes, the Bible decrees,
That there are laws of the land,
That we all should follow,
By God's graceful hand:
And we all should know,
That the law is not always right,
But there is one law,
That's precious in God's sight:
Jesus said it from the beginning,
That there is one law,
That should reign in our hearts,
And that is to love all:
For this only one law,
That God demands of us,
To love all of our neighbors,
Without one single fuss:
And this law only,
Is perfect in every way,
For God is this law,
Of love we experience every day:
For if you abide by this one law,
You will never fail,

For everything will line up,
Like a ship in its sail:
For we are OutLaws,
If only we heed,
To love like Jesus loves,
And to do what we read:
So let the Word of God,
In you become alive,
In actions and in words,
Let's let the love of God be our drive:

ENCOURAGING

One Passion

I only have
One single passion,
To have a hear,
Full of God's compassion:
I love my God,
And what He is to me,
He healed my heart,
And open my eyes to see:
He is my King,
And my Lord of Host,
And by His anointing,
I have the power of the Holy Ghost:
To Him I sing,
And to Him I live,
My heart, mind, and body,
To Him I give:
He is my air,
That fills my lungs,
And by His Spirit,
I speak in tongues:
He is my rock,
On which I stand,
He guilds and protects me,
By the might of His hand:
He is my peace,
In the midst of the storms,

In His image,
I was formed:
He is my joy,
In the battles heat,
He is my provider,
And covers my feet:
He is my light,
That shines in the dark,
He is my High Priest,
Who gave me His trademark:
He is my Shepherd,
Among the lambs,
He is my Father,
The Great I Am:
He is my Savior,
He's set me free,
He is my everything,
My passion to be,
God, I long to serve you,
For that's my compassion,
For it's my only desire,
And my one passion:

ENCOURAGING

Not by Works

No, I'm not living,
My very best,
But I trust God,
In Him I rest:
We're called heaven-bound,
By the blood of Jesus,
The hit the ground,
Even if we tried,
To live our very best,
We all fall short,
Of God's quest:
What I'm saying,
Is not a guess,
To live without Jesus,
Our lives become stressed:
It's not by works,
But by God's grace,
So fall to your knees,
And seek His face:
There's only one path,
To true salvation,
That's through Jesus Christ,
The King of the nation:
There's only one Lord,
And only one God,
Who can forgive your sins,

And spare you from the rod:
So ask Him in,
Before it's too late,
God will surely open,
The heaven's gate:
Repent of your sins,
And ask Him in,
Because that's the only way,
That you'll ever will win:
For He is the life,
And the only door,
So drop to your knees,
And pry to Him more:

ENCOURAGING

My Testimony: Will

Hi, I'm Will,
Just a simple man,
Sharing my testimony,
How God saved me in this land:
It was the year 1990,
And I was on the run,
My life was in shutters,
It truly was not fun:
I came to Lexington,
For I had no home,
Everywhere I turned,
I always stood alone:
I stayed at Salvation Army,
And I followed their rules,
I finally got me a job,
Which was so cool:
My job was in a mental hospital,
Called Eastern State,
I became a floor tech there,
And I carried a lot of weight:
Yes, I was a man,
Who had no face,
I was a big sinner,
who needed God's grace:
I knew nothing about love,
but everything about hate,

I knew nothing about peace,
just the chaos that I create:
I knew nothing about righteousness,
Only about sin,
I did not even know,
That I needed to be born again:
It was a normal spring day,
Off to work I went,
Not knowing this was the day,
That my life I would repent:
I went to my office,
And received my job details of the day,
I was to oversee a group of men,
And through the hospital show them the way:
They were subcontractors,
To update the bathroom stalls
My job was simple,
To keep the patients from entering the hall:
But every now and then,
I would unlock the door and take a peek,
They were praising their God,
On their knees and their feet:
They said not a signal word,
Every day when I took a sneak,
They were praising Jesus,
Through their singing and in their speak:
Now this went on for several days,
And my heart was drawn,
I finally seen the love of God,
And all fear was then gone:
They all testified to me,
And the Word of God they shared,

They told me Jesus loves me,
Yes, for me He cares:
I tried to defend my sins,
But the presence of God was too great,
So in the middle of that bathroom floor,
I met my destiny and fate:
Yes, it was in a bathroom,
Where I finally turned over my heart,
Jesus became my Lord and Savior,
And He gave me a brand-new start:
For this is my beautiful testimony,
That God can move anywhere,
And yes, He knows who you are,
For He knows the count of your hair:
If He can save me in a mental bathroom,
Where there are demons all around,
For there is no place,
That He cannot surround:
So it doesn't matter where you are,
Or who you are,
My God will save you,
Whether you're on earth or on a star:
There's no place He cannot reach,
So ask Him in today,
Because no matter if you like it or not,
Jesus Christ is the only way:
Just confess with your mouth,
And believe in your heart,
That Jesus is Lord and God raised Him,
And you, too, can have brand-new start:

ENCOURAGING

No, No, No, No, No

No, no, no, no, no,
No, no, no, no, no:

When the devil comes in,
Like the rushing wind,
Just tell him no,
We're born again:
For Christ has come,
And give us grace,
To say this word,
In the devil's face:

For Satan hear this word,
From my mouth,
Keep on traveling,
Beyond the south:
You have no right,
So I say this word,
In your ear,
I speak this word:

Yes, I am bought,
With the blood of Christ,
I'm no longer dead,
In Him I'm alive:
So I sing this song,
With this powerful word,
To tell, oh, Satan,
I whisper not this word:

No, no, no, no, no,
No, no, no, no, no:
    No, no, no, no, no,
    No, no, no, no, no.

ENCOURAGING

A Husband's Prayer

I write this poem,
To pray for my wife,
I pray the Word of God,
The giver of life:
I thank you, for in Genesis,
That you saw my need,
And by your holy Word,
I declare this my creed:
For you have said,
It is not good,
For man to be alone,
In this crazy neighborhood:
So from my rib,
You took from my side,
You made my woman,
Her I will never hide:
And from that day,
When she became my wife,
In all things of God's kingdom,
I no longer will strife:
For she is now and forever,
Bone of my bone,
And flesh of my flesh,
We're #1 seed sown:
And for this reason,
I leave Mom and Dad,

To cleave to my wife,
Which makes my heart glad:
And for this reason,
We two shall become #1,
#1 in mind, #1 in flesh,
In Jesus Christ the Son:
And Father God I pray,
In Jesus's mighty name,
That in _____, my wife,
Your kingdom forever reigns:
She is my Proverbs wife,
From chapter 31's book,
She is my rubies and treasures,
My heart she took:
For in her loins oh God,
Safely do I trust,
For she is my treasure,
Which will never rust:
She is my joy, oh, Lord,
She is all my love,
She is a gift from you, Father,
Who's sent from high above:
I thank you, Father God,
And I thank you, Lord,
That we will never break,
Our oaths, vows, and covenants,
For our own goodness sake:
So it doesn't matter,
Whether for good or bad,
We will always keep our oaths,
For that makes our hearts glad:
And we promise you, God,

We'll never put each other away,
For we are married for life,
Or until resurrection day:
And I thank you, Father God,
That her body belongs to me,
And I thank you, Father God,
She's the giver of my seed:
And I thank you, Father God,
That in the power of prayer,
That my body belongs to her,
For in this I do care:
Also, Father God, I thank you,
That she is my heart,
And no matter the distance,
Our love will never part:
And I thank you, Lord,
For her womb is so blessed,
And is so fruitful,
In this promise we'll rest:
And I thank you, Lord,
Our promises we'll keep,
Through prayer and fasting,
You we will always seek:
And I as her husband,
Do sanctify my wife,
By pleading the blood,
Of Jesus the Christ:
And I do stand in the gap,
For her each and every day,
And I bind that strongman,
From having his way:
I rebuke that strongman,

Of his evil hand,
By trying to destroy my household,
Of God's family plan:
For he cannot separate,
What God has put together,
It will always be my wife and I,
No matter the stormy weather:
For me and my household,
That my wife is good,
She is a godly woman,
Like your Word says she should:
And I thank you, Father God,
That _____, being my wife,
Who is the keeper of our home,
Who causes no strife:
And I thank you, Father God,
From me she won't run away,
But rather run to me,
In this glorious day:
For it is perfect love,
That casts out all fear,
And in your Holy Spirit,
Our love we hold dear:
And it doesn't matter,
If any deception or lies,
For perfect love covers all sins,
In God's holy eyes:
God we will always serve,
So get behind me, satan,
Our lives you don't deserve:
God I close this prayer,
For your Word I did speak,

For it will go out and accomplish,
That which I do seek:
So over my wife,
I pray these might things,
For by blood and water,
To us life brings:
So I give you glory, God,
And I give you all praise,
My wife is my glory,
Oh, Ancient of Day:
In all these things,
I pray in Jesus's name,
To the eternal God,
Who forever reigns:

I promise you, my wife,
        For I love you so,
        As I love own self,
        I'll never let you go:

ENCOURAGING
Prayer of #1

See in this very simple day,
I was trying to pray for just me,
But I was quickly corrected by God,
That it's no longer I but now is we:
Yes, I am a man of God,
Who has a heart and soul,
But in the vows of our marriage,
My wife makes our flesh whole:
See it was God who took from man,
The rib from his side,
And these two became #1,
As their two worlds collide:
She's rib from my rib,
She's bone of my bone,
She's flesh of my flesh,
She's my very own:
So when I pray for myself,
In my prayers I added my wife,
For if I heed not to Scriptures,
Then our home will fill with strife:
So in my prayers and supplications,
I also include my precious wife,
Because to do otherwise,
Our house will just become divide:
And if a house becomes divide,
How can that house stand

It slips off of solid rock,
Into the quick sinking sand:
So it's no longer just I,
Who's on this sailing ship,
But it's my wife and I,
Who the Lord does equip:
So in all of our prayers,
We pray in the power of God's Son,
Knitted together with my wife,
In prayer, we are #1:

ENCOURAGING
Global Warming

This is not a subject,
That is very hard or complexed,
It's also not a subject,
We should be stepping on peoples' necks:
Yes, you have your opinions,
And yes, you have your rights,
But tread not upon others,
In your personal global fights:
See there will always be,
Hurricanes in the sea,
Causing much harm,
To people like you and me:
There will be volcanos,
That will erupt and burst,
That flows out it's hot lava,
Like an evil curse:
And there will always be,
Earthquakes across the land,
Whether the land of the greens,
Or the land of the sand:
And there will always be,
Floods that arise,
Whether from the creeks or seas,
Or rain coming from the skies:
Here's the point,
That everyone needs to see,

That there is nothing we can do,
About the rising seas:
And there is nothing,
That we can do,
About the melting ice,
Of Greenland's dew:
See many on the left,
And many on the right,
Blames all of mankind,
To declare their rite:
See here is the truth,
There is nothing you or I can do,
About global climate warming,
Even if we turn ourselves blue:
Because it is written in the Word,
The earth is in morn,
Jesus said these things will come,
So we all have been warned:
If you don't believe me,
Then just look into the Good Book,
Matthew 24:6–8 or Luke 21:10–11,
For yourself take a look:
So like I said from the beginning,
The earth has been cursed,
By the sinful nature of man,
The earth for Jesus it thirst:
So until the Lord Jesus comes,
We all will just have to deal,
With all these weather patterns.

ENCOURAGING

America's Rebirth

There was a time,
Where we as a Nation,
Was focused on our family,
And the God of creation:
We stood in our schools,
And we pledged to our flag,
We carried respect,
Not just in our swag:
We prayed to God Almighty,
And our parents we honored,
We listened to our pastors,
The scripture we ponder:
There were less killings,
And there were no fears,
Nobody was assaulted,
Through sorrows and tears:
There was life in the playgrounds,
In the children's laugh,
There was life in the churches,
And in the school's staff:
There was life in the government,
And life in the streets,
There was life in everyone,
Whom you come across and meet:
But those days are over,
Because death has entered in,

People started becoming crazy,
Through their self-centered sin:
Now there's more murders,
And hate across the land,
Where everybody is your enemy,
So strike then down by your hand:
For they all are racist,
And everyone is insane,
And we kicked God out,
Even Jesus and His name:
And there are many illusions,
And tons of rapes,
There are no superheroes,
We all wear our own capes:
But there is a remnant,
That God has kept around,
Who prayed for this Nation,
That in God's Spirit we would drown:
And in God heard those prayers,
And God heard their cries.
And soon there will be a revival,
Where God opens the skies:
Yes, I'm taking about,
God coming *back in*,
In the rebirth of America,

And forgive this Nation from sin:
It's always been His will,
And it's always been His plan,
To rebirth America,
With His mighty hand:
And we as a Nation,
Will be His people again,
And there will be harmony,
With our enemies and kins:
For God is a god of love,
We will see this by the cross,
And there will be much salvation,
Given among the lost:
So, Father in heaven,
Let thy will be done,
As it is in heaven,
Through Jesus your Son:

ENCOURAGING

I'm Coming Home

I have many,
Brothers and sisters,
We have many names,
Even been called as critters:
We are all over the world,
In many different branches,
Some of us are at war,
While others are on ranches:
There is the coast guards,
Who serve in the seas,
These brothers and sisters are awesome,
Who serve you and me:
There is the Navy,
There is the Air Force,
And none of them serve,
In the spirit of remorse:
There is the Marines,
There is the Army,
Yes, we are dads,
And yes, we are mommies:
We are daughters,
And we are sons,
We carry swords,
And we carry guns:
We are sisters,
And we are brothers,

We are here to serve you,
As well as all others:
We serve in war,
And we serve in peace,
Here in this land,
And even overseas:
This is our heart,
And we answered the call,
We have seen,
Brothers and sisters fall:
We serve all of America,
And honor our flag,
We serve without race,
In that we brag:
We stand as one,
We stand all together,
We stand united,
In all conditions and weather:
One way or another,
In mourn or groan,
We say to our loved ones,
That we're coming home:
And to all those who have fallen,
This we do decree,
We honor all you soldiers,
In this land and overseas:
God bless our troops…

ENCOURAGING

I Am Declaration

I am cleansed and white as now from all sin:
I am faithful to follow the commandments of love:
I am humble before God and, therefore, mankind:
I am blessed in heaven and on earth:
I am God's, and He is mine:
I'm not of myself I belong to Him:
I am a child of God, and Jesus is my King:
I am a seed of Abraham and so are my children:
I am purchase by the blood of Jesus,
I am over all the animal kingdom by my rites:
I am an overcomer of fear and failure:
I am more than a conquer over satanic powers:
I am redeemed by the blood of Jesus:
I am justified and righteous in God my Father:
I am perfect in Him and made in His image:
I am healed from all sickness by faith:
I am blessed coming in and blessed going out:
I am anointed to do God's work:
I am fruitful and multiply in much:

Listen, my friends,
The Bible has a lot to say,
That you are many, many things,
Because Jesus is the truth, life, and way:
Read the Bible,
While you still can,

Find out what it says about you,
In this evil and dying land:
So be not deceived,
Open your heart and eyes,
And be one of the I Ams,
And reach beyond the skies:
So get right while you can,
Yes, I'm speaking to you, my friend,
For the rapture of the church,
Is right around the bend:
Yes, there is still hope,
His name is Jesus Christ,
Accept Him as your Lord and Savior,
And with the church you'll arise:
Now for those who are left behind,
For you it's too late,
But let me share this truth to you,
On how our God is still great:
Just because hell is now released,
Don't ever give your hope away,
Stand firm in the Lord,
For Jesus is coming for you one day:
Just decree the "I Am" declaration:

ENCOURAGING

He Is Declaration

He is Lord,
He is King of kings,
He is Unfailing Love,
He is the Word, which is Right and True,
He is the Maker of heaven and earth,
He is the Deliverer of all those who trust Him,
He is the Healer and our Protector,
He is the Rescuer to the helpless,
He is the Savior and the Redeemer,
He is the Healer and the Teacher of purity,
He is the Clothes to the broken-hearted,
He is our Fighter in a world of chaos
He is our Friend to those who are His,
He is the Brother who are in His family,
He is the Lawyer who stand in judgment,
He is Righteous in life and Mighty in manner,
He is the Justice of fire against the lawless,
He is the Fountain of life for those who seek salvation,
He is the Great Light in a world full of darkness,
He is the Many Waters to all those who thirst,
He is the One who has me on His mind all the time,
He is Merciful to the world unrighteous Nations,
He is Eternal who is worthy of all praise,
He is the all Powerful One,
He is the Cleanser of all my sins,
He is the Wisdom and full of all knowledge,

He is the Engraver who has my name in His hand,
He is the Refuge for the oppressed,
He is God who is highly exalted above the heavens,
He is the Written Stature and trustworthy,
He is Right in all His prospects,
He is the Captain of our soul who makes whole,
He is the Alpha and the Omega beginning to end,
He is Jehovah the God who meets our needs,
He is the Commander and Chief,
He is the Ordinance of holiness,
He is the Great I Am who will never be a shame,
He is the Lion of the tribe of Judea,
He is the Savior of the world who paid the price,
He is the Author and Finisher of our life,
He is Jesus Christ God Himself,
He is my Declaration:

ENCOURAGING

Ghost in the House

There are many people,
Who claim what they see,
That there are ghosts,
And this is what they believe:
They say there are some,
Of relatives of the past,
Some of them are kind,
While others do harass:
They say that these ghosts,
Know secrets that are hidden,
That only their relatives would know,
But this communication is forbidden:
Because now I'm going to speak truth,
That there is no such thing,
As family friendly ghost,
And the tunes that they sing:
The Scriptures tells us,
That when a person dies,
That they go to heaven,

Or to hell they fly:
I'm not trying to be insensitive,
But this is not a lie,
There's no such thing as family ghosts,
Once a person does die:
Yes, what I'm saying to you,
These are demonic forces,
And they want you to believe them,
To hears their evil voices:
These family friendly ghosts,
Are sent from hell,
And their only one job,
Is to get you under their spell:
The Bible calls these ghosts,
Familiar demonic spirits,
This isn't about your emotions,
Whether you don't want to hear it:
For Jesus Himself said,
That they will come as angels of light,
And in their darkness they desire,
And in their darkness they take delight:
So if you are dealing,
With these devilish demons,
Rebuke them in Jesus's name,

So you'll stay a free man:
For there is power,
In Jesus's blood,
To cover you from head to toe,
Like a mighty flood:
So rebuke that ghost,
From all your house,
And let the Spirit of God,
For God is not a Mickey Mouse:
For God is the God of truth,
And He is the life,
Let go of them familiar spirits,
So you no longer have to strife:
For God wants you,
To communicate with Him,
To live an abundant life,
And with peace, fill your brim:

ENCOURAGING

Generation Everyone

There is a generation,
That's vast in our land,
It's a mighty move of God,
That He's directing by His hand:
He's sitting a higher flame,
A fire within our heart,
It's the releasing of His Spirit,
Truly a heavens glorious spark:
Their calling is great,
It's a wonderful thing to see,
Their anointing by Jesus,
For this thing shall be:
They'll prophecy in truth,
For in Him they will flow,
They'll point you to Jesus,
For their fruits you'll know:
They'll cast out demons,
In Jesus's mighty name,
They'll move in God's authority,

The world will never be the same:
They'll lay hands on the sick,
And people shall surely feel,
The power of our God,
For healings will be sealed:
They'll raise up the dead,
Demand them back on their feet,
They'll do all these things,
For Jesus sits on the seat:
Oh, there's a mighty generation,
Who flows in God's gifts,
Their out to make Him famous,
And they will always uplift:
Their focus on purity,
And their eyes are set,
Their passion toward God,
They're no longer satan's pet,
For they are sons and daughters,
People who are set free,
They are everyday people,
People like you and me:
Oh, there's a mighty generation,
That are here in the now,
We confess Him a Savior,

And to our knees we give Him bow:
We are filled with His Spirit,
And the gospel we preach,
And with the love of the Jesus Christ,
With the purity of God's Word,
All the lost we will reach:
And there is no age bracket,
So if you are here in the now,
You're a part of this generation,
His move you will endow:
For this mighty outpouring,
Is for Generation Everyone,
It's for every man and women,
And for every daughter and son;
So take part in this revival,
It's the greatest harvest of all,
It's not only your duty,
But it's part of your call:

ENCOURAGING

Come as You Are

Oh, come as you are,
No matter if you are near or far,
For my Jesus will always be there,
Whether you have long or short hair:

Just come as you are,
No matter if you are near or far,
For sin has no more sting,
Because Jesus is King of kings:

So come as you are,
No matter if you are near or far,
Your redeemed by His blood,
Come under the cleansing flood:

Come as you are (every boy and girl)
No matter if you are near or far (man or woman)
For He has come just for you,
To make you a chosen few:

So come as you are,
No matter if you are near or far,
For Jesus died for you,
So be a chosen, chosen few:

Oh, come as you are,
No matter if you are near or far,
Oh, come as you are,
No matter if you are near or far:

ENCOURAGING

Dance in the Fire

Dance in the fire,
It takes you higher,
Jesus is the Lord,
The King of kings:

Jesus is the Lamb,
Who sits on high,
Dance in the fire,
It takes you higher:
Jesus is the Lamb,
Who was sacrifice,
Dance in the fire,
It takes you higher:

Jesus is the Lord,
Who was crucified,
Dance in the fire,
It takes you higher:
Jesus is the One,
Who sets you free,
Dance in the fire,
It takes you higher:

ENCOURAGING

Bloodline

It's in our Bloodline,
To be like Him,
It's in our Bloodline,
To serve the Great I Am:
It's in our Bloodline,
To be born again,
It's in our Bloodline,
To be free from sin:
It's in our Bloodline,
To answer the call,
It's in our Bloodline,
To conquer all:
It's in our Bloodline,
To walk in healing,
It's in our Bloodline,
By faith not by feeling:
It's in our Bloodline,
To rule in this land,
It's in our Bloodline,
To show God's hand:
It's in our Bloodline,
To be as royals,
It's in our Bloodline,
To be completely loyal:
It's In our Bloodline,
To be kings and queens,

It's in our Bloodline,
To be Christ clean:
It's in our Bloodline,
Because Jesus did bleed,
It's in our Bloodline,
Be He is our every need:
It's in our Bloodline,
To be daughters and sons,
It's in our Bloodline,
Because the cross has *won*:

ENCOURAGING

Blessed Salvation

Blessed Salvation,
Jesus Christ,
Blessed Redeemer,
Jesus Christ:

Blessed Salvation,
Jesus Christ,
Blessed Redeemer,
Come alive:

Blessed Salvation,
Jesus Christ,
Blessed Redeemer,
Jesus Christ:

Blessed Salvation,
Jesus Christ,
Blessed Redeemer,
Come alive:

> Jesus needs to come alive in me,
> Jesus needs to come alive in me,
> Jesus needs to come alive in me,
> Jesus needs to come alive in me:

Blessed Salvation,
Jesus Christ,
Blessed Redeemer,
Jesus Christ:
Blessed Salvation,

Jesus Christ,
> Blessed Redeemer,
> Come alive:

ENCOURAGING
Abortion

This is a subject,
That many may call hate,
It's about the life of a child,
Who Baal tries to take:
It's also a subject,
That may seem very hard,
But the truth I speak,
Your life may become ajar:
Let it be very clear,
That God's Word stands on its own,
And He doesn't answer to you,
Because He sits on the throne:
So here is the truth,
The Bible make it clear,
It doesn't care about your emotions,
Or the feelings you hold dear:
God's Word is final,
And it has lots to say,
That the killing of babies,
Is not God's way:
Many fleshly women,
Say their bodies are their own,
So they commit this abortion,
But death they have sown:
They declare that their above God,
They declare it's their rights,

But the killing of these babies,
Are sickening in God's sight:
This poem can go on and on,
It can go all through the night,
But, ladies, here is the truth,
Your bodies you have no rites:
Your bodies were created,
By God's living hand,
So you belong to Him,
While you're in this land:
This poem isn't written,
To hate or condemn,
But it is written,
So you'll listen to Him:
I close this poem,
With these final thoughts,
If you are born again,
Then your life has been bought:
So this sin or any other,
Has no power over you,
You are a new creation in Christ,
Covered by God's dew:

ENCOURAGING

I Give

Bless your glorious name,
Oh, Lord, my Savior,
For you have coated me,
With your Holy Ghost flavor:
For you are honored and holy,
Oh, yes, Lord, you are,
For your truth is much brighter,
Than the universe's biggest star:
For I give you glory,
Oh, Lord Jesus Christ,
For your anointing in me,
Who God has risen:
And I give you all praise,
Oh, King of kings,
And I declare your Word,
For you are my everything:
Blessed, honorable, and holy,
Glory and praise,
To the Lord God Almighty,
The ancient of days:

ENCOURAGING

I Give You, Lord

I give you glory,
I give you praise,
I give you honor,
All of my days:

I give you power,
I give you reign,
I give you all, Lord,
In Jesus's name:

I give you glory,
I give you praise,
I give you honor,
All of my days:

I give you power,
I give you reign,
I give you all, Lord,
In Jesus's name:
    In Jesus,
        In Jesus,
            In Jesus's name:

ENCOURAGING

I Hear a Sound from Heaven
A Prophetic Word (2017)

I hear a sound from heaven,
It's like a rushing mighty wind,
I see people all over the world,
Becoming born again:
I hear the Spirit of the Lord say,
There's a revival in the land,
There's a mighty move of My Spirit,
And there's a mighty move of My hand:
There will be great miracles,
And there will be much healings,
The move of My Spirit,
Will break through the ceilings:
And there will be much deliverance,
And My people will be set free,
From the strongholds of bondage,
Their chains will no longer be:
And the power of My anointing,
Will cause My people have dreams,
And the power of My anointing,
Will rush in like a mighty river stream:
And I will break the yokes of darkness,
Off the people's necks,
And I will pour out My blessings,
And satan's tactics I wreck:
Young men will have visions,

Thus, saith the Lord,
And the power of My presence,
Will unite the church in one accord:
For I am the Lord God Almighty,
Who brings revival across the lands,
And I am the Lord God Almighty,
Who reaches beyond heavens spans:
And I will call unto Me,
A new set of people,
And I will fill them with My Spirit,
And make them My temple:
For this mighty move of Mine,
Will be loud and clear,
I will draw the old and the young,
To Me they will draw near:
And I will raise up the young,
To take a mighty stance,
And I will pour My power in them,
And I will cause then to dance:
They will be greater than Elijah,
And they will be greater than David,
Through My mighty power,
Sin and evil will be raided:
For thus, saith the Lord,
There will be a mighty sound,
And the stronghold of satan,
I will crush to the ground:
I hear a sound from heaven,
It's a rushing mighty wind,
I see a revival in our land,
And the lost becoming born again:

ENCOURAGING

I'm the Broken Clay

Oh, Lord, you are the potter,
I am the clay,
Mold and make me,
This is what I pray:
I lay myself down,
Before your mighty hand,
To form me in your image,
As I walk through this land:
I know in my heart,
That there will be many tears,
But break me down to nothing,
And shatter all those fears:
The chains of darkness,
As it appears,
Has drowned me in pain,
And has sickened me for years:
So break me into ashes,
Back into the ground,
And add to me your Spirit's water,
So that I may abound:
Stretch and pull,
Yank and tug,
And where those cracks and holds are,
With your Word do plug:
Then pressure cook me,
With your righteous heat,

And chip away all those extras,
And let them all fall at your feet:
As the clay sets still,
Cooling on the dry racks,
Awaiting for my Potter's touch,
To reveal any other cracks:
As the pot shines and glisten,
And now ready to paint,
This is where the transformation take place,
The clay becomes a saint:
As the potter builds the character,
Forming the details in the clay,
He's clearing the path,
For us to walk in each day:
So you as the clay,
Represents its maker,
Release for His purpose,
Whether a dish, cup, or salt shaker:
So, guys, shine His light,
Because you are His pot vessel,
Show your handy work oh God,
So the flesh cannot wrestle:
Again, oh, Lord my God,
I am the broken clay,
Mold me and form me,
For this is what I pray:

ENCOURAGING

Jesus and Me

I have walked,
This road alone,
Until I receive,
The Son on the throne:
And through the battles,
They have been hard,
Jesus has been there,
My life He has guard:
wherever I am,
My God is there too,
And brought me salvation,
And called me as one of his few:
So I'm no longer alone,
We walk hand in hand,
For Jesus and I walk,
Together in this land:
So on this day I declare,
That it will always be,
My wonderful Savior,
My Jesus and me:

ENCOURAGING
Love and Obedience

Many of us have heard,
This little saying a lot,
But in its connections,
We have just not sought:
For there is no separation,
In Obedience and in Love,
Their tied in together,
As we serve God above:
When it comes to the Word,
And when we say we love,
We have to align ourselves,
Even if we get shoved:
And when it comes to Obedience,
We must all understand,
That this is a heart's attitude,
As we walk in this land:
For if you cannot see,
That these two are one,
Then you'll never understand,
How a hot dog fits a bun:
So how can we say,
That in Obedience we obey,
If we walk not in Love,
In God's perfect way:
And in like manner,
How can we all say,

That Love we live every day,
If we do not obey:
Here's the point my friend,
You can't have one without the other,
For these two make a team,
That's true my sisters and brothers:
To love the Lord God Almighty,
Is to walk to Him in Obedience,
And always do remember,
That Love is the ingredient:
So obey the Lord God Almighty,
And to always walk in Love,
For this fits all sizes,
Like hand in glove:

ENCOURAGING

More and More

You are my pillar,
You are my healer,
You are the one,
Who sets me free:

You are my pillar,
You are my healer,
You are the one,
Who maketh me:

More and more,
More and more,
I confess,
I need you, Lord:

More and more,
More and more,
I confess,
I need you, Lord:

So let my prayer,
That your light will be on me,
So that the whole world,
In me, you they see:

ENCOURAGING
Mortals to Immortals

Let's start with this,
That we all came from dust,
Some came through love,
While came through lust:
Even in that fact,
God always has a plan,
And no matter who you are,
He always has you in His hand:
Yes, God breathes His life,
Into the particles of the earth,
And you are not a mistake,
For He controlled your birth:
Back to the point,
You are a spirit,
That resides in the flesh,
Even if you don't want to hear it:
From the very beginning,
We were made in His image,
To live forever,
In His very lineage:
Yes, the snake did come,
To offer man to sin,
And that's when death,
To take life within:
See just like God,
Immortals we were called,

But now we are mortals,
Because of Adam and Eve's fall:
So we are at a place,
Where everybody will die,
And depending who your master is,
Will determine whether you go low or high:
So whether you go to heaven,
Or if you go to hell,
Immortal you will become gain,
That place you'll forever dwell:
So if I were you,
I would get your life right,
By accepting the Lord Jesus Christ,
For He is the true light:
The choice is up to you,
Which road you want to take,
For God made you to be immortal,
For He makes no mistakes:
So live your mortal life,
For you have a free will,
To become immortal,
By the blood Jesus spilled:
So accept Him as your Lord and Savior,
For Jesus is the only way,
To come unto God the Father,
So ask Him in today:

ENCOURAGING

My God Is a Big, Big God

My God is a big, big god,
    My God is a big, big god,
My God is a big, big god,
    My God is a big, big god:

He's bigger than the mountains,
He's bigger than the hills,
He's bigger than the devil,
And anything he spills:
He's bigger than the valleys,
He's bigger than the seas,
He's bigger than you,
He's bigger than me:

My God is a big, big god,
    My God is a big, big god,
My God is a big, big god,
    My God is a big, big god:

ENCOURAGING

The Lord's Prayer

Jesus the Son said,
"That this is how we should pray,
To our Father in heaven,
In this manner in this way:
Our Father in heaven,
Hallowed be your name,
Let your kingdom come,
For it is you who reigns:
And as it is in heaven,
Let your will be done,
For we glorify you,
In the name of your Son:
And God give us this day,
Our daily bread,
Feed our hearts and spirits,
And cover our heads:
Ad forgive us of our sins,
As we forgive those who sin against us,
Lead us not into temptation,

For in God we trust:
For thine is your kingdom,
And thine is the flower,
And thine is your glory,
Forever in this hour:
Amen and Amen:"
(Matthew 6:9–13)
So here's the point,
When you pray,
Pray this prayer,
Each and every day:
Keep it simple,
Keep it clear,
When you pray this,
God will surely hear:

WORD

Sacrifice of Christ

This poem maybe graphic,
But it has to be said,
About the Son of God,
Whose blood was shed:
It all started with a kiss,
On the night of the feast,
This crowd of angry people,
Including scribes and priest:
After they found Jesus guilty,
Through their lies of sin,
Bearing false witness against Him,
Their courts could not win:
So they took Him to Pilate,
And he washed his hands from their plan,
And he handed Jesus over,
To the evil people of the land:
For their hearts were greatly evil,
As they chanted and sung their song,
Crucify Him, crucify Him,
Though He did nothing wrong:
Then the soldiers came in,
And took Him to the marketplace,
Where they mocked Him greatly,
By beating and punching His face:
As they cursed and spat on Him,
They made Him a crown of thorns,

Stripping our Lord Jesus make,
For His cloths they have torn:
For they said, "Who's this king of glory?"
As they place the crown of thorns on His head,
Pressing it down deeply,
That His forehead began to bleed:
As they tied His feet,
With whips of glass and bones,
His body they began to beat:
And as flesh was ripped away,
At the sound of the mighty whips,
The sorrows and the pain,
Jesus's back began to split:
And after this demonstration,
They forced Him to His feet,
And placed a heavy cross upon Him,
To carry through the streets:
As He dragged and struggled,
His people began to weep,
As splinters from the cross,
In His skin went in so deep:
He finally got to the location,
Where there was a mighty hole,
They slammed His cross in it,
As they placed Him upon the poled:
They pierced His loving hands,
With nails made of steel,
They pierced His loving feet,
Oh, the pain was so real:
As He hung there for many hours,
A soldier with a long spear,
Pierced the side of His body,

Because Jesus they all feared:
And when the hour came,
Jesus finally died,
God's precious blood,
Flowed from His side:
Drip by drip,
His blood came flowing down,
Bringing man unto salvation,
As His blood came to the ground:
The earth did quake,
As in heaven and hell,
It was in that powerful moment,
Where God tore the vail:
And it was here at Golgotha,
Which is known as Mt. Skull,
It was here ladies and gentlemen,
Where Jesus died for all:
For God so love the world,
That He gave His only Son,
That whosoever believes on Him,
Their salvation can be one:
For no greater love than this,
That He laid down His life,
And died on that cross,
And became the sacrifice:

(Matthew 27:11–66)

WORD

Armor of God

Today as I rise,
From my night's rest,
In the armor of God,
I do get dress:
I first out on,
The *Helmet* of *Salvation*,
To renew my mind,
From being in starvation:
Then I put in place,
Upon my chest,
The *Breastplate* of *Righteousness*,
That makes me the best:
And on my waist,
The *Belt* of *Truth* is placed,
The *truth* sets me free,
So I can run my race:
Then here it comes,
Upon my very feet,
The *Gospel* of *Peace*,
Which makes me meek:
Then the *Shield* of *Faith*,
Which quinches every dart,
I will take it up,

To guard my heart:
In my right hand,
Is the *Sword* of the *Spirit*,
The living Word of God,
Can you hear it:
So each and every day,
Put His armor on,
So in the heat of the battle,
You'll know how to respond:
So be that godly soldier,
A soldier of light,
Who's ready and dressed,
To stand and fight:

(Ephesians 6:10–18)

WORD

Ask, Seek, and Knock

Here's the secret of prayer,
For there's much to be said,
Some letters in black,
And some letters in red:
We know about the Lord's Prayer,
We know about prayer and fasting,
We know it's all done by faith,
In believing what we are asking:
Here in this verse,
Jesus made it plain to see,
That many of us are lacking,
Because we don't use the key:
For He keeps it very simple,
For this is what He said,
So open up your Bibles,
And eat your daily bread:
He said ask in my name,
And it shall be given,
For your not the God of the dead,
But the God of the living:
And when you go out to seek,
You shall surely find,
For all of His promises,
He'll surely give to thine:
And when you go knocking,
He shall open up the door,

And cover you with My Spirit,
For I am God your Lord:
For everyone that receiveth,
Is because they ask,
And it is by their faith,
That these things shall pass:
And to everyone that findeth,
Is because they did seek,
For they came to me as children,
So humble and meek:
And every door I open
Is because My people knocked,
For all My blessings,
Will remove the stumbling block:

Ask, seek, and knock:

(Matthew 7:7)

And you'll never be weak:

WORD

By Faith

By faith,
Are all things hoped for,
By faith,
We trust in the Lord:
By faith,
Are the things not seen,
By faith,
Is the evidence redeemed:
By faith,
Him we do seek,
By faith,
God does speak:
By faith,
God meets our needs,
By faith,
God blesses our seeds:
By faith,
We are born again,
By faith,
We're cleansed from sin:
By faith,
Righteous are we,
By faith,
God we will see:
By faith,
We reap and sow,

By faith,
In God we grow:
By faith,
He's given us the land,
By faith,
All the promises of His hand:
By faith,
He blesses the womb,
By faith,
He's coming back soon:
By faith,
We're not under the law,
By faith,
Came down Jericho's wall:
By faith,
Is what it is all about,
By faith,
Give your victory shout:
By faith,
He's given us riches,
By faith,
We stay out of ditches:
By faith,
His promises we obtain,
By faith,
We stand in Jesus's name:
By faith,
We quench the violent fire,
By faith,
He takes us higher:
By faith,
Hell we do escape,

By faith,
He clothes us in His cape:
By faith,
We are now free,
By faith,
Heaven we will see,
By faith,
We are now saved,
By faith,
Christ rose from the grave:
By faith,
Death can't give,
By faith,
The just shall live:
By faith,
Heaven is near,
By faith,
Rebuke all fear:
By faith,
The strongman is bound,
By faith,
We stand on solid ground:
By faith,
We are healed,
By faith,
We're Holy Ghost sealed:
By faith,
All things are done,
By faith,
All battles have been won:

(Hebrews 11:1–40)

The point of this poem,
Is crystal clear,
Without faith,
God cannot draw near:
For it is impossible,
God to please,
Without faith,
Showing through our deeds:

WORD

Death to Resurrection

There rose a great multitude,
On the night of the feast,
The chief priest and scribes,
The very embodiment of the beast:
They sought to destroy Jesus,
And at every corner and turn,
Through the kiss of betrayal,
This is what we have learned:
They took Jesus as their prisoner,
As they held their religious courts,
Bearing false witness against Him,
Telling lies of all sorts:
The chants of the people,
Have been heard loud and clear,
So they delivered Jesus to Pilate,
Because is death they wanted dear:
As they continued in their lies,
Pilate gave them their pick,
To release the King of the Jews,
Or to Barabbas would they stick:
And as their voices became one,
They cried, "Crucify, Crucify,"
Yes, crucify, crucify,

Crucify, Jesus God's Son:
They declared Jesus
To be crucified,
So Pilate released Jesus,
To these people of lies:
These people made a cross,
For Him to carry in the streets,
His body became bloody,
As they yelled and screamed:
As they made Him a crown of thorns,
Mocking the King of kings,
As His clothes they did tore:
They took Him to Golgotha,
Which is known the place of skull,
They nailed His hands and feet,
To be crucified before all:
The King of the Jews,
They wrote upon the cross,
He hung there for hours,
Just to save the lost:
And when the ninth hour came,
The will of God He chose,
He cried unto God the Father,
As He gave up the ghost:
And the veil of the temple,
Was ripped in to the two,
From the top to the bottom,
This is what Jesus came to do:
Then they took His body down,
After the earth did shake,
And all those who stood by,

Their hearts began to quake:
And God sent Joseph,
Took Jesus to is grave site,
And clothe Him in fine linen,
All clean as pure white:
Then the chief priest and scribes,
Word lived in their fear,
Proclaimed to block the door,
So His body won't disappear:
And as Jesus did speak,
Time and time again,
That three days later,
Death did not win:
Just as prophesied,
No matter what these say,
The tomb was empty,
For the stone was rolled away:
And there at the tomb,
Two angels one on each side,
Said unto Mary and those,
Why do you sorrow and cry:
For the Lord is not here,
Come see for your eyes,
For our Lord Jesus Christ,
Is risen and *alive*:

(Matthew 15, 16)

WORD

Great and Marvelous

Revelation 15:3–4

Great and marvelous
    (Repeat) Great and marvelous,
Are thy works,
    (Repeat) Are thy works,
Just and true,
    (Repeat) Just and true,
Are thy ways,
    (Repeat) Are thy ways,
For thy King of the saints,
For thy are King of kings,
And Lord of everything:

Who shall fear thee,
    (Repeat) who shall fear thee,
And glorify,
    (Repeat) and glorify,
Thy name,
    (Repeat) thy name,
For thy are holy,
And all worship before thee,
Thy King of all kings:

Revelation 15:3–4

WORD

Isaiah 61:1–7

The Spirit of my Lord,
As anointed me,
Is preach the good news,
For all to see:
He has sent me out,
To bind up the brokenhearted,
To bring God's healings,
To those who are discarded:
And to release the prisoners,
From darkness of sin,
To bring God's life,
To the spirit within:
To proclaim their life,
In the Lord God's favor,
To show them the truth,
Of Jesus our Savior:
To comfort all who mourn,
In heart and in tears,
To serve God only,
Throughout their living years:
To give them a crown,
instead of ashes,
To give the oil of joy,
To all the masses:
To give a garment of praise,
instead of despair,

We're oaks of righteousness
By the power of prayer:
For He has called us all,
To be royal priests,
To be ministers of our God,
In Him we'll increase:
So receive our double portion,
Instead of our shame,
We're no longer a disgrace,
In the power of Jesus's name:
For this is our God,
To display His Splendor,
To call us to salvation,
No matter what your gender:

(Isaiah 61:1–7)

WORD

No More Monsters

Ghosts that hunt,
And disappear on a dime,
You shadow in your evilness,
Your no family of mine:
Goblins, you creatures,
Thinking your full of wit,
Causing death to your enemies,
If I were you, I would quit:
Witches who hex,
And witches who curse,
By the blood of Jesus,
Your spells are reversed:
Snakes that crawl,
And hiss to bring fear,
I'm filled with the Holy Spirit,
To me you can't draw near:
Werewolves that howls,
With their sharp claws,
I'm protected by God's Word,
So read that clause:
Vampires who roam the night,
Thirsting for a single bite,
Know my blood is holy,
Because I'm filled with God's light:
Demons who take,
Know you lost the war,

Because the more you attack,
The more I praise God even more:
Mummies that are wrapped tight,
With no skin to bone,
You're a laughable joke,
'Cause all you can do is moan:
Clowns with your face decked up,
With your belly showing,
Your pedophile thoughts,
Here will no longer be growing:
Zombies of the dead,
You people of the grave,
I live in everlasting life,
Because Jesus's life He gave:
Chucky that crazy little doll,
With his knife he does his killings,
But I have the Sword of the Spirit,
Who cares about his feelings:
Orco, you thing you are all that,
You think you're so strong,
Strength only comes through Jesus,
So that makes you totally wrong:
And lasting is satan,
Who thinks he's winning,
But he's like a sick little dog,
In Jesus, I am grinning:
So Ghost and Goblins,
Witches and Snakes,
Werewolves and Vampires,
And Demons who take:
Mummies and Clowns,
Zombies and Chucky the Doll,

Orco and Satan,
Upon Jesus's name I call:
You all are defeated,
Because Jesus did bleed,
And by the Word of God,
You all have to flee:
You all are powerless,
So to my words take heed,
The Blood of Jesus Christ,
Over my life I decree:
So no more monsters,
Under my bed,
And no more fear,
Running through my head:
For I belong to God,
The greatest power of all,
Every one of you monsters,
To your knees you have to fall:
For it is written,
That every tongue shall swear,
And every knee shall bow,
That Jesus Christ will be declared:
(Romans 14:11)

WORD

Spirit of the Lord

For on this day,
I praise my God and Sire,
For I'm baptized in Him,
By water and fire:
As it was written of old,
but now is my decree,
That the Spirit of the Lord,
Is now upon me:
For He has anointed me,
With the gospel to preach,
And in its tremendous power,
The world I will reach:
I'm now anointed,
To set the captives free,
To heal the brokenhearted,
And make the blind to see:
And to those who are bruised,
To show them heavens key,
For where the Spirit of the Lord is,
There is liberty:
For this is acceptable,
The year of our Lord,
For by His Word and Spirit,
We stand in one accord:

(Luke 4:18–19)

WORD

The Ministry Gifts

The Scripture says,
There is only one,
One body, one spirit,
One God the Son:
One Lord, one faith,
One hope of the call,
One truth, one baptism,
One Father of all:
And it is He,
Who's above all:
And through all,
And in you all:
And he has given grace,
To every man,
A measure of the gifts,
By Christ's hand:
And here in the Scripture,
We can see a list,
Of the anointing Christ,
Of the ministry of gifts:
To some He gave,
The *Apostle* call,
To build His church,
And knock down the wall:
There are *Prophets*,
He did give to some,

To reveal His truth,
Under this sun:
And He gave some *Evangelist*,
To declare His heart,
To show His love,
So salvation won't part:
And to others,
He gave the *Pastor's* call,
To be their shepherd,
So the sheep won't fall:
Then there's the gift,
Of being *Teachers*,
Searching out Scriptures,
For all the seekers:
For all these gifts,
Are to perfect the saints,
To edify the Body of Christ,
In the water's banks:
For deep calls out to deep,
Till we all become one,
In faith and knowledge,
Of God the Son:
So do not despise,
These ministry gifts,
Because if you do,
The anointing you'll miss:

(Ephesians 4:4–16)

WORD

The Tunnel of Thoughts

In this poem,
I would like to share,
A truth about the mind,
That we all have to bear:
Because of sin,
We all were born,
Into a godless life,
Each has our own thorn:
But when Jesus came,
And died on that cross,
Through His holy blood,
We are no longer lost:
So once we're saved,
By asking Him in,
We are no longer sinners,
But now we're born again:
But there is still,
A battle within the mind,
That we have to renew,
All the time:
So here are the Scriptures,
If the tunnel of thoughts,
That we must think on,
Because our lives have been bought:
On these things,
We should think,

What is *true*,
So we won't sink:
And on these things,
Have thoughts that are *honest*,
Praising God,
His Word admonish:
Think on these things,
Thoughts of *just*,
Worshipping God,
Is a must:
And think of things,
That are *pure*,
Stay in faith,
So you'll endure:
Think of these things,
That are *lovely*,
And in His love,
He'll keep you cuddy:
And think of things,
Of *good report*,
Because as you do,
All your troubles He'll sort:
And if there be any *virtue*,
And there be any *praise*,
Think on these things,
Glorifying the ancient of days:
Think 'bout the *peace* of God,
Which passes all,
Shall keep your hearts,
In Christ Jesus stand tall:

(Philippians 4:7–8)

WORD

Two Masters

Jesus spoke this parable,
So the people could understand,
That there are two masters,
Who dwells within this land:
So let's take a look,
And see what Jesus has spoken,
First, we have mammon,
Who does a lot of choking:
The Bible call him satan,
Who's out to make his steal,
He's a thief in the night,
Yes, folks, satan is very real:
And it is in his mission,
To kill and destroy,
It doesn't matter people,
If you're a girl or a boy:
Then Jesus also spoke,
About the greatest master of all,
And that is God Almighty,
Which we shall serve and fall:
For it is Him alone,
Who can destroy all human life,
But He gives you the choice,
To have peace not strife:
So back to the point,
That Jesus was making,

That there are two masters,
That do the shaping:
So pick which master,
Because you can't love both,
You chose righteousness,
Or in your sins be clothed:
So if I were you,
The Lord God I would love,
And hate the other master,
And serve God who sits above:

(Matthew 6:24)

WORD

You're the Salt

When you become saved,
By asking Jesus in,
You became the salt of the earth,
By being born again:
Wherewith shall it be salted,
If the salt loses its flavor,
But to be cast out and trodden,
Because the salt lost its Savior:
And in your salvation,
You're now a city of light,
Which cannot be hidden,
Because you shine so bright:
So take your light,
And do not hide,
By putting it under a bushel,
Or casting it aside:
So all before men,
Let your light do shine,
Glorifying your Father,
Until the end of time:
Remember, Jesus is the Savior,
In which the salt needs,
So stay within His Spirit,
And to His Word always heed:
(Matthew 5:13–16)

WORD

Blessed Are They

For Jesus said,
Blessed are the poor,
For in the spirit,
Theirs is the kingdom of God more:
And blessed are they,
Who do mourn,
For they shall be comfort,
For thus God has sworn:
And blessed are the meek,
For truly they shall,
Inherit the earth,
Because before God they shall bow:
Blessed are they,
Who hungers and thirsts,
After His righteousness,
God will fill until they burst:
And blessed are the merciful,
For at the end,
They shall obtain mercy,
Because their born again:
And blessed are they,
Who are pure in heart,
For they shall see God,
From the very start:
And blessed are the peace makers,
For they shall be called,

The children of God,
In Him they'll never fall:
And blessed are the persecuted,
For righteousness sake,
For theirs is the kingdom of heaven,
Who makes no mistakes:
And blessed are you,
Who stand at the stake,
When evil is against you,
For My namesake:
Be exceeding glad,
And rejoice in joy,
For your reward is heaven,
To every girl and to every boy:

(Matthew 5:3–12)

WORD

Speak the Word

Forty days,
Forty nights,
Jesus fasted,
Then began the fights:
Jesus was hungry,
And the devil came in,
And tried tricking Him,
To cause Him to sin:
The Word of God,
The tempter spoke,
Trying to cause Jesus,
To fold and choke:
"If you're the Son of God,"
He said unto thee,
"Turn these stones into bread,
So everyone can see:"
But Jesus replied,
"By bread alone,
Man shall not live,
But from the words of God's throne:"
Then the devil took Him up,
Into a holy city,
And said, "Cast thyself down,
For God will how pity:
For He has given angels,
In charged over thee,

Against dashing thy foot,
To make you fall or fled:"
But once again,
Jesus did speak,
"Tempt not the Lord thy God,
For He alone holds my feet:"
And once again,
The devil took Him to a mount,
Showed Him the glory,
Of all the kingdoms about:
And he said unto Him,
"Fall and worship me,
And all of these kingdoms,
I will give unto thee:"
And Jesus with power,
"Satan, I rebuke you,
I only worship my God,
You devilish punk:"
The point of this poem,
When the tempter comes in,
Speak God's Word,
And you will always win:

(Matthews 4:1–11)

ABOUT THE AUTHOR

Will lives in Conneaut, Ohio, where he resides with his family. He received Jesus as his Lord and Savior in the spring of 1990. He began his journey as an evangelist then became a youth pastor after moving on from Christ to the Nations Bible Institution. He now serves the body of Christ as an evangelist and prophetic minister. He is known for his written songs, prophetic teachings, and for his poetry. His passion is for both nonbelievers and believers to be blessed in their journey in life.